Deck the Halls

Quilts to Inspire Family Traditions

Lynda Hall

Deck the Halls

Quilts to Inspire Family Traditions

By Lynda Hall

Editor: Donna di Natale
Designer: Bob Deck
Photography: Aaron T. Leimkuehler
Illustration: Eric Sears
Technical Editor: Kathe Dougherty
Production assistance: Jo Ann Groves

Published by:
Kansas City Star Books
1729 Grand Blvd.
Kansas City, Missouri, USA 64108

First edition, first printing

ISBN: 978-1-61169-067-5
Library of Congress Control Number: 2012946849

Printed in the United States of America by Walsworth Publishing Co., Marceline, MO

To order copies, call StarInfo at (816) 234-4636 and say "Books."

Table of Contents

Dedication...4
Acknowledgements...................................5
About the Author.....................................6
Introduction...8
General Instructions...............................10
Sources...73
Templates..74

Projects
Christmas Wreaths.................................13
Chilly...21
Chilly's Big Brother................................27
Santa's Route..37
Christmas Packages...............................45
Christmas Goose.....................................51
Bridging the Gap....................................59
Behind the Log Cabin............................67

Dedication

I feel very blessed to be surrounded by the people I love and the friends I've made over the years. I am dedicating this book to my sister-in-law, Donna Phillips. She was the one who introduced me to quilting, taught me to quilt and has followed my progress from the beginning. She has been my friend and sister-in-law for over 43 years. We have the best time together stitching every week and bouncing ideas off each other. What I find to be fun is that we both love the same fabrics and style of quilting; yet, we see color a little differently so when our projects are finished they do look different. We make projects for each other, time permitting, and enjoy surprising each other with a new fun item.

I would also like to dedicate this book to all the wonderful friends I've been able to meet since I started quilting. Traveling to quilt market has enabled me to meet so many talented quilt designers who I admire and have become friends with. Teaching at quilt guilds and doing trunk shows around the country has enabled me to meet delightful people whom I stay in contact with a lot. To all my *Back Door Friends Pattern Club* members who have followed my quilt line from the beginning... they are so very special to me. And lastly, to the friends I've made through various avenues of the Internet world. This has been and continues to be a wonderful tool for meeting people across the waters. Yes, it's a very small world indeed when it comes to computers.

My dad always told me, it's not *WHAT* you know, but *WHO* you know that can make all the difference in what you can accomplish. My dad died at the very young age of 54, but was very instrumental regarding how I feel about things today. Life is so very short and something we should embrace each day to the fullest.

Acknowledgements

As a child I remember my parents instilling in my sister and me how much a "please" and "thank you" mean. Appreciation of help given is so important. With that thought in mind I'd like to say thank you to the following people:

To my husband of 43 years, Curtis, who has always encouraged my creative endeavors. Thank you for always being there and understanding how creative juices flow! I love you very much!

To Donna Phillips, my sister-in-law, for stitching two of the projects in this book: Christmas Wreaths and Christmas Goose. Your work is always wonderfully done and I appreciate you so very much. Thank you!

To Katherine Christenson, machine quilter, who not only did her special magic on all the quilts, but also taught me more about machine quilting than I ever knew. Katherine's motivation isn't just to complete the quilt — she cares about what she does, and that really shines through. I'm so glad we met. Thank you!

My gratitude also extends to everyone at Kansas City Star Quilts who was involved in putting together this book. I wish I could have been there a second time to see how all of you operate, but please know you have made me look wonderful with all your help and expertise.

Thank you Doug Weaver and Diane McLendon for allowing me to share my favorite time of year with everyone.

My Editor, Donna di Natale — my newest kindred spirit — who has been a joy to work with on this book. I'm so glad we've had a chance to work together and I look forward to getting to know you better.

Photographer, Aaron Leimkuehler, who has certainly proven himself to me. Aaron also did the photography on my "A Little Porch Time" book. He continues to amaze me with his skill.

Tech Editor, Kathe Dougherty. Kudos to you for doing what I think is the hardest job of all — keeping my less than average love of math correct.

Designer, Bob Deck, who has captured my feelings of Christmas and has made the presentation very special.

Artist/Illustrator, Eric Sears, for taking my templates and making them perfectly correct.

Photo stylist, Edie McGinnis, who has been my quilting friend for many years now. We certainly have fun together. Photographing a Christmas book in June takes a special team to make that happen. Thank you!

Photo Production Manager, Jo Ann Groves — thank you for making each of the photographs come to life for my favorite holiday.

About the Author

Lynda Hall
Business: Primitive Pieces by Lynda

Born: November 26, 1949
London, Ontario, Canada

In 1952, the family moved to Orlando, Florida, where Lynda attended school.

Married in 1969
She and her husband moved to Apopka, Florida, in 1973 and continue to live there now.

Married – 43 years to Curtis Hall
Children – 2 wonderful sons; Bryan and Chad; 1 wonderful daughter-in-law, Lane, who is married to Chad; 2 granddaughters: Rebecca and Sarah; 1 grandson: Cade (Happy Gramma!).

Lynda has no formal training or degrees. She is mostly self-taught in her creative accomplishments. She was raised by two loving parents with a strong belief that, "You can do anything you want to if you only try!" She has raised her children with the same belief.

Before she had children, Lynda worked in finance as a private secretary for the president of Coca Cola -- Plymouth, FL division, and in the insurance field. When her children were born she wanted to be a hands-on mom so worked from home in sales and taught painting.

Lynda has always loved creative endeavors. She taught oil painting for 15 years in various art studios and from her home. Working with color doesn't change from paint to fabric so it wasn't much of a change from painting to quilting.

She was introduced to quilting in 1992 by her sister-in-law. The very first thing she ever quilted was a wall hanging called Hopscotch designed by Little Quilts … what goes around comes around, as they say, because Little Quilts now sells Lynda's patterns.

Carol Crago, owner of Good Home Quilt Company, Lynda's local quilt shop, encouraged her to design quilt patterns and so she started her own quilt designs in 2000. **Primitive Pieces by Lynda** was born two years later (2002) and to date there are 84 quilt patterns and 3 books in her line. Her first book, **Primitive Youngins**, was self-published; the second book, **A Little Porch Time**, was published by Kansas City Star Books.

Lynda has designed projects for the Meredith Corporation magazines, *American Patchwork and Quilting, Quilts and More* and its specialty magazine, *Sew Scrappy,* over the years.

Lynda has created projects for *Primitive Quilts and Projects* magazine since it started in 2011. Her granddaughter, Rebecca, helped design the first project, "Cold Days," and both Rebecca and Sarah worked on the "Wabbits" project. Look for more projects coming soon.

She loves history and admires women from her Gramma's era, who didn't have much but accomplished so much with the little they had. Each pattern in this book has a fun story about a family member or event.

Because Lynda is a person who likes to have fun, all inset seams have been taken out of her patterns. They are scrappy quilts, and have larger pieces. She doesn't worry much about corners that don't match and/or points that come up missing. She thinks they might be having a party on the back!

You can visit Primitive Pieces by Lynda online at http://www.primitivepiecesbylynda.com, or read her blog, http://www.primitivepiecesbylynda.blogspot.com. She can also be found on Facebook under her pattern company name: Primitive Pieces by Lynda.

Introduction

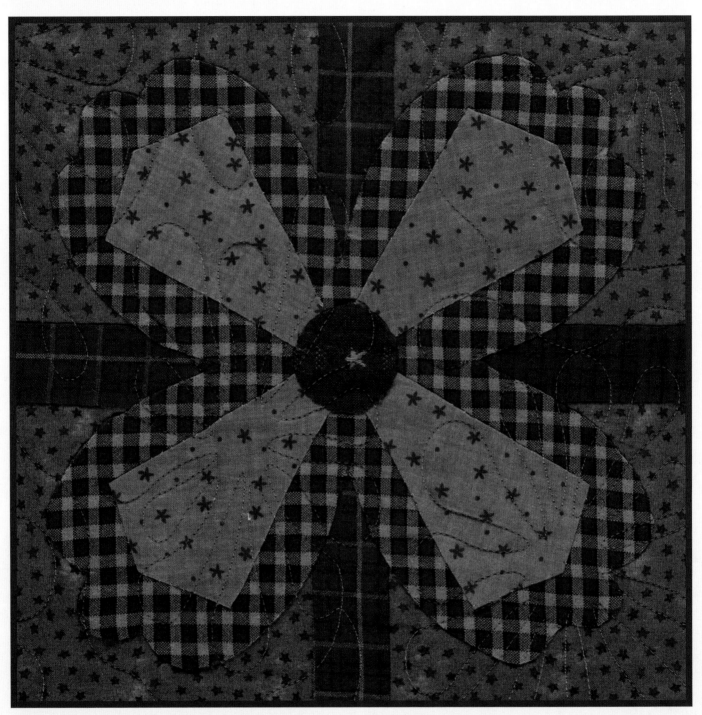

Cold blustery days, snow on the ground, bundling up to go outside, rubber boots, coats, scarves, hats and such are not what I know about living here in the South. I was born in London, Ontario, Canada, but when I was three-and-a-half years old our family of four moved to Florida. I've lived here for 60 years. One thing is for sure — I do know about sand. We all do the same things around the holidays no matter where we live, but I think here in the South we work a little harder to get the spirit of the holiday in our homes. I decorate 13 to 15 Christmas trees inside the house, each having their own theme, and have dozens of my favorite holiday decorations in every room — Santas and snowmen are grouped together to make it more festive. The porch usually sports a few poinsettias, a favorite snowman that lights up, and of course, a few more trees. Paw hangs the outdoor lights upstairs on the roof and along the porch on the bottom. What is it about lights that make them so festive?

Decorating usually begins early here for me. It takes a little time to get it all together. All the primitive trees I have come in around the first part of November. It gives me time to get all the lights on each tree. We always go the day after Thanksgiving to get our real tree. We've had some beauties over the years ranging from 8- to 13-feet tall. After the lights are on that tree as well, I get all the ornaments out. I have some very fun old glass ornaments that usually are on the tree in our bedroom. My granddaughters help decorate some of the smaller trees. It's always fun to see how they arrange them. I've never changed what they do. I just smile when I look at them. We have a 6-foot tree in the loft that has a lot of homemade ornaments on it along with others I've purchased. It has a vintage yo-yo garland on it, too. I have some animated Santas I put on a tree in the downstairs bedroom. When plugged into the white lights on the tree they each move. My boys always enjoyed them while they were growing up here at home. I have some large primitive ornaments I've collected over the years that usually are put on our real tree. They always make me smile. I have a 6-foot tree that gets all kinds of rusty tin ornaments on it. Another 6-foot tree that has smaller primitive ornaments on it also goes in the living room. Homemade fabric garlands adorn those trees and there's usually a fun tree topper that isn't always a star on top.

What I've learned over the years is that it's not where you live, but what's in your heart that makes any holiday special. I love Christmas Day because our entire family comes to our house for a sit-down dinner. We're all so very busy that we don't get to see each other a lot during the year. It's a time to reflect, regroup and have tons of fun. We've had as many as 26 here when everyone can make it home. I think we number around 31 at the present time, so this year should be even more fun.

I hope you enjoy viewing and making the quilts being offered in this book. Traditional Christmas is red and green, but I wanted to share with you that primitive country quilts don't have to be the norm. Since I usually start decorating for Christmas early in November, when it's still actually Fall, I thought that a Christmas Wreath quilt would be fun to start with. Red, green, orange and black seemed quite fitting. Made first it could carry you from fall through the Christmas Holiday.

Christmas Goose is the meal my gramma would have cooked for her family, so a quilt reflecting that seemed right to me.

As we get nearer to when Santa might come along, a quilt showing the route he might take to get to all of us seemed in order. Santa usually brings presents that are placed under the tree, so why not have a quilt representing that?

And then, after it's all said and done, our red and green turns into Valentine's red and white ... so I really thought it would be appropriate to have a quilt that still seems a little Christmas but could be used for our very first holiday after the New Year. This quilt is actually reversible, with a green/cream/black log cabin on the back. Yes, that's right ... St. Patrick's Day is still in that cold, wintry time of year. So, from the fall of the year all through the winter, I hope you have enough to keep you busy. Ask your friends to join you on one of those winter days ... you can cut and stitch and have your own quilting bee.

People are always surprised when they learn where I live because of the color palette I use for my quilts. I'm not a light and bright kind of person at all. And, of course, having said that, I have to remind everyone that we all use the same colors in our quilts, it's just mine are usually darker on that value scale.

General Instructions

Fabrics

Since we all use different colors, the ones used in my quilts are the values I like the best. To make quilts that are special to each of us, we should use the color values we love -- and, scrappy is always going to be my favorite. Using a variety of values always make things interesting. When I say use light yellow or cream, this means you can choose any shade you like on the lower end of the yellow value scale. The same applies to middle value yellow (tan/brown) and/or dark yellow (dark brown) ... each is a value of yellow. By using the values you like the best, your quilt will become your own and special to you.

Borders

When adding borders, it's important to remember to ALWAYS measure across and down through the middle of your quilt to get an accurate measurement. One of my favorite methods is to lay the quilt top across my table in my sewing room. The sides can hang down over the edge because it's the middle of my quilt where I want to be getting a measurement.

After getting a ballpark figure I stitch together enough border pieces (I most always make a scrappy border) and press the seams open. I lay my quilt top on my cutting table face up, my border strip face down across the middle starting at the left hand side edge, flatten it out across the middle. You don't want to pull it too tight, but make sure it's laying flat. At the other side, cut it right at the edge and you have your first border. I do this with each border I add, including the last border.

Post Blocks

Post blocks can be another problem, so I've taken the problem away by not putting one in each corner. Remember, we quilt to have fun and if we get stressed out about a project it almost never gets finished.

Adding one post block is easy. Stitch it to the end of a border strip and then trim that border at the opposite end. Adding a second post block is again easy. If you go around your quilt just add another post block to that border strip and do the same trim at the other end.

The third post block can be done the same. That leaves one corner without a post block and to me, this makes it a fun looking quilt.

Another thought about post blocks is ... do they really need to be at the outside corners? Why not in the middle of the strip? Or perhaps offset on each side so they just don't match up? You will see this in some of my quilts ... now you'll know why.

Finished size vs. cutting size

It might seem silly not to know the difference, but know that when the pattern says the quilt is 40" x 50" that doesn't mean that is what you cut. Look for the block size in the directions. This should also be the finished size, so again, remember that the cutting instructions will be one number and the finished size will be different. A 12" finished block means it should 12 ½" before you sew the blocks together.

Seams, corners, points

Each of these items should be accomplished as accurately as you can. However, having said that, let me remind you that we should be having fun while we are making a project. I might un-sew something one time, but if it goes back in the same as the first time it's saying to me, "leave it alone and move on." I don't get stressed out about this much. In the state of Florida there are no quilt police coming to take you away.

Backing

You will notice that in each of the quilt projects the amount of yardage for the back is not listed. I love piecing the back, whether it's by using left over fabric from the quilt I'm working on, or just using up some of my stash that goes with the quilt. There is an example of this on page 19. Here's a simple way to make backs for your quilts. If the top measures 59" x 72" you can bet the back will have to be that plus 12" (6" for each side and 6" for the top and bottom) so that the machine quilter can add it to her frame and do her magic. The main thing to remember is that this should be fun!

Projects

It's during the fall of the year when I get really excited about decorating the house for my favorite holiday – Christmas. A wreath on the front door and several around the house inspired this quilt. The circle shape is just perfect. Traditional Christmas is green and red, but adding a little fall into the mix, especially when it's still autumn, makes sense to me. This quilt could be the first one to be hung on my railing up in the loft. I hope you enjoy making this all-time favorite Dresden block into a quilt you can put out in the fall and enjoy all the way through the Christmas holidays.

Let me introduce you to...

Quilt Size: 64 ½" x 77"
Pieced/appliquéd blocks 12" finished

Christmas Wreaths

Designed by: Lynda Hall | **Stitched by:** Donna Phillips
Machine Quilted by: Katherine Christenson

Gather together the following items to make this quilt:

FABRIC AND SUPPLIES
* 4 yards assorted oranges for background squares and outer borders
* 1 ³/₈ yards assorted greens for the Dresden pieces in blocks
* 1 ³/₈ assorted reds for Dresden pieces in blocks
* 1 ½ yards assorted black print for block centers, inner sashing, inner border and 3 post blocks

Templates A and B on page 74.

Let's get started:

BLOCKS

Cut 20 – 12 ½" assorted orange squares for your background blocks.

Cut 12 – Red Template A pieces for each block (240 total for 20 blocks).

Cut 12 – Green Template A pieces for each block (240 total for 20 blocks).

Cut 1 – Black Template B piece per block (total 20 for 20 blocks).

Sew together 12 red and 12 green Template A pieces alternating the colors to complete one Dresden circle. Make 20 of these.

Pin these onto the 20 orange 12 ½" background squares – you should have at least ¼" around the outside edge to sew the sashing on when you have completed the appliqué.

Appliqué the outside edge of this circle, leaving the inside unstitched. You do not need to turn under the inner part of these Dresden pieces because the black center will cover it up and it will be less bulky.

Place the black template B piece in the center and appliqué around the outside edge.

NOTE: To find the center, fold the block in half both ways (horizontal/vertical) and pin. Do the same with your circle (template B) match up the folds and you will have your circle in the middle.

SASHING

You will have both vertical and horizontal sashing between the blocks and rows of this quilt.

Cut 15 – 1" by 12 $\frac{1}{2}$" strips from the various blacks for the vertical sashing between the blocks. Sew the blocks together with 4 blocks and 3 sashing strips per row. Sew a total of 5 rows.

Cut 4 black strips – 1" x 51" – one each to go across the entire width of the 4 blocks you have already sewn together. I like my sashing scrappy so I sewed 2 or 3 – 1" strips together to make up the 51" length. Sew a sashing strip between each row of blocks. Refer to the quilt assembly diagram for placement.

INNER BORDER

Cut 1 $\frac{1}{2}$" strips of assorted blacks for the inner border that will go all around the quilt center with no post blocks.

Be sure to measure across and/or down through the middle of your quilt to get an accurate measurement for each border you add.

Sew the strips together and cut the side, top and bottom strips according to your measurements.

OUTER BORDER

This border is orange with black post blocks. Cut 7" wide strips of assorted orange fabrics and stitch them together. Measure across and down through the middle of your quilt to get an accurate measurement for all the borders. Stitch the top and bottom borders on. The other two will be for the sides.

Cut 4 – 7" x 7" black post blocks for all of the corners. Sew a post block onto each of the remaining pieced border strips. Find the middle of the side of your quilt and the middle of your border strip and pin in place. Pin the corners in place and the rest will fit in nicely. Pin along the strip and stitch it down.

Quilt, bind, and enjoy.

Personally I like the look of only one or three post blocks on a quilt instead of framing the entire quilt by them.

NOTE: If you only add 1 and/or 3 post blocks measuring is easier. Start at the top of your quilt, measure across the middle of your quilt to get an accurate measurement … without a post block, stitch this piece to the top of your quilt. Measure the length of your quilt down through the middle, including the first border. On the right side of your quilt, add a post block to one end of a border piece. Cut to length and stitch it on. When you get to the bottom, sew a post block to another border strip. Measure again, across the middle of your quilt, including the bottom border you just stitched on. Cut the strip to this measurement and stitch in place. For the last side, add yet another post block to the remaining border strip. Measure the length of your quilt including both top and bottom borders to get an accurate measurement, then cut and stitch the last side border in place.

ASSEMBLY DIAGRAM

BACKING

The back of this quilt was pieced together using reds, greens, oranges and blacks left over from the front of the quilt. You can piece your back or not. Just have fun doing it your way …

I hope you enjoy making your Christmas Wreaths Quilt. I'm going to hang mine out during the Fall to usher in my Christmas holiday. Thank you so much, Donna, for stitching this wonderful quilt so that all the family will be able to enjoy it on Christmas Day.

I think the story of Frosty the Snowman has lived in all of our hearts for years...but, did you know that in the South, it's usually Chilly that we see most often, especially in my primitive part of the country? I live in central Florida and our weather is cool or chilly, at best, most of the winter season.

Chilly is a special friend of mine. He shows up most nights in the winter, but then disappears during the day when our temperatures climb. He'll keep the chill out of the house and he's really fun to look at. Just hang him on a doorknob and he'll do the rest. I hope you enjoy making this project for your home and that you'll think of all of us in the South when you feel a chill in the air ...

Let me introduce you to ...

Size 7" x 9"

Chilly

Designed and Stitched by: Lynda Hall

Gather together the following items:

FABRIC AND SUPPLIES

Wool Scraps (I don't use white at all and try to find wool that is really grayed down and mottled):

- ❄ 7 ½" x 9 ½" piece of black tweed wool
- ❄ Fat eighth - olive green for 3 trees – two large and one medium sized
- ❄ Scraps of middle value yellow-brown for tree trunks
- ❄ 2" x 9 ½" piece of light yellow-cream for bottom
- ❄ Scraps of light yellow wool with a blue tinge for snowman parts – front and back – You can cut Chilly as one piece or as individual pieces like I did. I liked that he looked a little disjointed.
- ❄ Scraps of black for hat and tree ornaments
- ❄ Scraps of purple for the year and hat stripe
- ❄ Scrap of middle value orange (burnt sienna) for 2 noses
- ❄ Scrap of dark yellow (brown) for arms
- ❄ Scrap of middle value yellow (gold) for star

- ❄ 2 different sized buttons for his eyes
- ❄ 7 ½" x 9 ½" black/tan check homespun with a red stripe – or fabric of your choice for the back
- ❄ Dream cotton stuffing – use enough to plump up the door hanger.
- ❄ A 10" to 12" piece of twine for the hanger
- ❄ Thread – black, olive green, purple, light yellow (cream), middle value yellow (gold), dark yellow (brown), orange

    NOTE: Whatever thread you like to use is fine. Use thread that matches the item you are sewing down. I like Weeks Dye Works cotton thread the best on small items and on larger items I like to use wool thread - Aurifil, Genziana and even pearl cotton.

- ❄ Glue – a glue stick works fine, but use what you like best to hold the items in place.
- ❄ Template plastic or freezer paper – I cut these shapes free hand, but use the method that works best for you.

Now, let's get started!

Cut 1 – 7 ½" x 9 ½" piece of black tweed wool as your background.

Cut 1 – 2" x 9 ½" piece of the cream wool you've chosen for the ground and place it along the bottom. I did not cut away the tweed from the back, but you can after you stitch the ground on if you like. You can have it straight across or at a slight angle like mine. You decide.

Trace the templates on pages 75-76.

Cut out all the shapes on the lines (*note: you do not have to add any seam allowance with wool; however, if you choose to make Chilly out of fabrics you will need to add ¼" seam allowance to all the template pieces*).

FRONT

Lay out the trees, snowman including his arms and nose, hat, and star on your background.

When you are satisfied with the placement of these items, dab a little glue on each to hold in place and stitch each item down.

Cut the date out of the purple wool and sew it on the left tree. Add the black dots for the ornaments on both trees.

Stitch on the two different buttons for his eyes and make them just a little off kilter.

Stitch x's for his mouth. I included two French knots in two places because he has a sweet tooth.

Stitch the 5 buttons on his front (I made small squares out of dark yellow (brown) wool and put some straight and some on point to look like diamonds.

Stitch his arms on as shown – it kind of looks like he's taking a bow.

When you have appliquéd all the pieces to the front, it's time to add the back.

BACK

Trace and cut one tree trunk, 1 partial snowman, and 1 orange nose. Remember to cut on the drawn line.

Cut the fabric you've chosen for the back – 7 ½" x 9 ½".

Stitch all the way around, right sides together, leaving no opening.

Cut a slit in the backing material at least 3" long, slightly off center and to the left.

Turn right side out and stuff with the dream cotton stuffing until you are satisfied with the results. You want it to be firm, but not overstuffed. You want him to hang flat on a doorknob or drawer pull.

Once you are satisfied – stitch up the opening with a whipstitch.

I don't know if I told you, but Chilly has a friend. I've never been introduced to this friend because he has always been hiding behind a tree. I wonder who it could be?

Use the other large tree you cut for this space.

Appliqué these items onto the back of your project to cover up where you whip stitched the opening closed.

If you remember, Chilly likes to hang around so, keeping this in mind, I added a piece of twine so that he can hang on a doorknob and/or cupboard knob. To do this, cut a piece of twine approximately 10-12" long. Tie a knot in each end. You can stitch each end on the back, about 1 ½" in from each side leaving the knot on the outside, or you can open up the top put the knot inside and hand stitch it closed. Either way works just fine. Hang him on the doorknob closest to the outside door so that he'll feel the cold when the door is opened. Snowmen need to feel the "chill" once in a while so that they won't melt all over your floor.

I hope you enjoy making my friend and that you'll enjoy him all through the winter. Maybe he'll even introduce you to his friend!

25

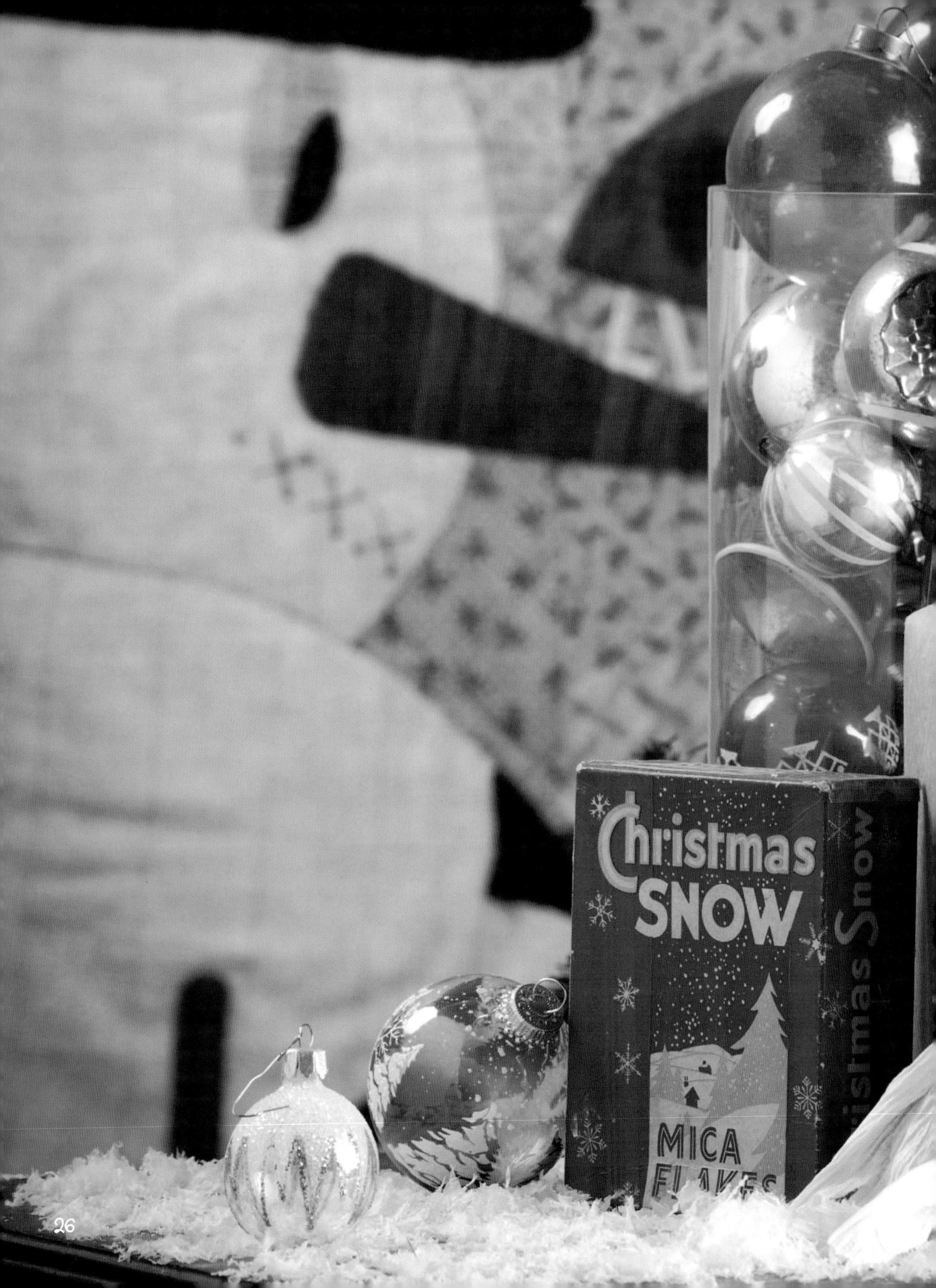

Christmas
SNOW

MICA
FLAKES

On the back of the Chilly pillow you'll notice another snowman hiding behind a tree. I thought he was just being shy, but that wasnt the case. He was just waiting for me to make him special for all of you. He happens to be Chilly's Big Brother, who wants to be part of the holiday season, too.

Having seasonal pieces to display around the house is so much fun. They are quick and easy to make, and they brighten up a table, a small wall space, or even a door!

I have a barn wall in my kitchen that my husband made for me. The door has a push/pull handle that covers the entry to my pantry. It's a perfect place to hang a project such as this. Since this guy has been so patient with me to bring him to life, he's going to love being the center of attention this Christmas.

Let me introduce you to...

Finished Size: 23 ¼" x 69"

Chilly's Big Brother

Designed and stitched by Lynda Hall

Gather together the following items and let's get started:

FABRICS AND SUPPLIES

Cotton:
- ❄ 2 yards assorted creams for the background
- ❄ 2 yards of a cream print for the back – you could also piece the back like you've done the front.
- ❄ ½ yard assorted green and red stripe for binding – approx. 195 inches

Wool:
- ❄ 1 ¼ yards cream colored wool for the snowman
- ❄ 3 – 6 ½" squares for large snowflakes
- ❄ 2 – 5" squares for middle-sized snowflakes
- ❄ 1 – 4" square for small snowflake
- ❄ 1 – 9" cream square for the 3 candy canes
- ❄ Scraps of red for stripes on the candy canes OR you can stitch these on using red pearl cotton
- ❄ 1 fat quarter green plaid for the tree
- ❄ 3" x 10" orange stripe for nose
- ❄ Scraps of cream for eye (this should be slightly darker than his body)
- ❄ Scraps of black for eyes
- ❄ 7" x 10" black for hat
- ❄ 1 ½" x 6 ½" plaid for hatband
- ❄ Scraps of red for berries on his hat
- ❄ 2 different greens for holly on his hat, each 2 ½" x 6" – can also use for star on stocking
- ❄ 2 – 3 ½" x 4 ½" pieces blue for birds
- ❄ Scraps of dark yellow (brown) for the bird wings
- ❄ Scraps of cream for the bird legs
- ❄ 9" x 24" piece red wool for stocking
- ❄ 2" x 8 ¼" multi plaid for stocking cuff
- ❄ Scraps of multi plaid for the numbers (2 5)
- ❄ Scraps of cream for stripes on stocking
- ❄ 6" x 12" piece of multi plaid for letters (D E C)
- ❄ 2 – 8" x 8" pieces of dark yellow (brown) for gingerbread boys
- ❄ Scraps of black for their eyes
- ❄ Scraps of black for 3 belly button triangles
- ❄ 14" x ½" dark yellow (brown) for long arm
- ❄ 6" x ½" dark yellow (brown) for short arm
- ❄ 4 ½" x 4 ½" orange plaid for mitten
- ❄ Black pearl cotton and/or wool thread for mouth

- ❄ Freezer paper and/or template plastic
- ❄ Marking pencil – I used Roxanne's Quilters Choice pencil – white
- ❄ Threads: wool, pearl cotton, and regular cotton threads the color of the pieces you are stitching down

BACKGROUND

Build the background piece first. I pieced an assortment of light yellow fabrics (creams) together to make my background. A diagram is enclosed for you to see, but no sizes have been included. It's just to show you a way to make the background. I love the way different fabrics pieced together add texture to your background.

Cut your background pieces into strips the same width for each row. Then cut the strips into different lengths so that each row doesn't match up. You can even make a triangle out of one square — see down at the bottom in the center row.

Sew the rows together. Trim to measure the overall size — 23 ¼" x 69".

Note: this size fits my door perfectly. However, if your door is a little longer or a little wider ... make it to fit yours.

NOTE: another option for the background would be to use only one piece of fabric if you choose to make it that way.

When the background is completed, make a quilt sandwich by layering the backing (this can also be pieced, but I used one fabric for the back), batting and your pieced top. I used 505 spray adhesive to hold the layers together, then machine quilted it on my sewing machine. I used a white pencil to mark diagonal lines, 2" a part, first one way, stitched these on my machine, and then marked lines going the opposite way and stitched those. This gives you a diamond shaped quilting pattern when you are done.

Note: I quilted the entire background, even behind the snowman because from the back it would have presented a big area of no quilting.

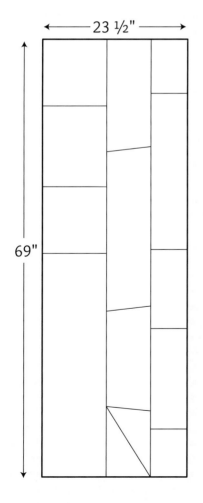

APPLIQUÉ

When you have finished quilting the background it's time to cut the wool pieces. The templates, except for the tree, are on pages 77-88. For the tree, cut 1 ½" strips of varying lengths and refer to the placement guide. Feel free to add or subtract to the objects to make the quilt yours.

When you are satisfied with the placement of all the pieces, it's time to stitch them down.

I use regular cotton thread when stitching down small objects. I love the assortment of colors Weeks Dye Works has in their collection the best. I use wool thread — Aurifil and Genziana are my favorites — to stitch down the larger objects. Use thread closest to the color of the object you are stitching down.

What's really fun about wool appliqué is that you don't have to turn anything under. I use a primitive stitch (see sidebar on page 34) around each piece. I use a blanket stitch around the outside edge when I am sewing both the front and back pieces together when they are both wool.

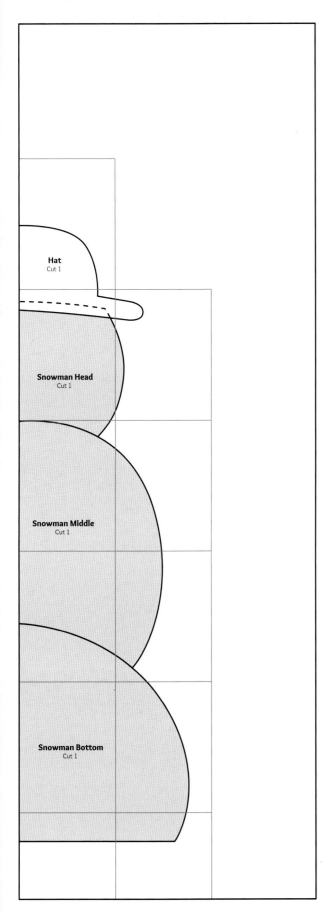

Snowman Template
Assembly Guide

Assembly Guide

33

PRIMITIVE STITCH

Some people refer to the "primitive stitch" as a "whip stitch"... but, to me it's more like an upside down blanket stitch. Where a blanket stitch has a thread that runs around the outside edge of the piece you are sewing down, in the primitive stitch that outside thread is going to be down at the bottom between the appliqué piece and the background piece. Here's how I do it:

1. Start by threading the needle and tying a knot at the end.

2. Come up between the piece you are appliquéing and the background where you want to start your stitching.

3. Keep the thread straight (dotted line) as shown below.

4. From that point, where the thread is to go back down catching the background fabric bring the stitch over to the left ¼" and up through the appliqué piece you are sewing down. Make this stitch at least ¼" in from the outside edge. By keeping the thread really straight, your stitches will be straight. If your thread is not straight, the next stitch you make will be at an angle.

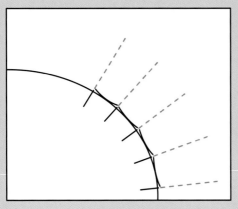

Fig. 2

34

BINDING

Once your appliqué is completed, cut 2" strips of green/red stripe cotton fabric and sew them together. Fold in half, press and stitch your binding on. You have a great door hanger for the season. ... Oh, yes, I do believe you could get this one done before Santa comes this year.

Merry Christmas everyone!

I hope you track Santa's route on Christmas Eve like I do. Our local TV channels help by letting me know where he was last spotted. It's always exciting to me to know exactly where he is and how long it will take for him to get to our house. Yes, I know, I've been told I'm the biggest kid there is when it comes to Santa, but I strongly believe that as long as there is giving in the world there will always be a Santa. It was that thought that inspired the creation of this particular quilt. I thought the blocks, sewn together, looked like a neighborhood.

Let me introduce you to...

Quilt Size: 65" square
Block Size: 12" square finished

Santa's Route

Designed and stitched by: Lynda Hall
Machine Quilted by: Katherine Christenson

Gather together the following:

* 2 ³/₈ yards assorted greens
* 2 yards assorted light yellows (creams)
* 1 ⁵/₈ yards assorted reds
* 1 ⁷/₈ yards assorted blacks

Because these blocks are on point, you will make three different sized blocks. The main components of each of these are the same; however the triangles on the half blocks and corner blocks will have their own measurements.

WHOLE BLOCKS
Make 13

For each of the whole blocks cut:
* 4 black 4 ¼" squares per block for the corners
* 1 black 3 ¾" square for the center
* 20 red 1 ¼" squares
* 24 light yellow/cream 1 ¼" squares
* 8 green 1 ⁵/₈" x 4 ⁷/₈" strips per block
* 8 light yellow/cream ⁷/₈" x 4 ⁷/₈" strips per block
* 4 red ⁷/₈" x 4 ⁷/₈" strips per block

Let's get started...

Start by assembling the different parts of the whole block.

Sew 5 red and light yellow/cream 1 ¼" squares together alternating colors, then sew it to the right hand side of the 4 ¼" black square.

Sew together 6 red and light yellow/cream 1 ¼" squares, alternating colors, and sew this to the bottom of the piece you just made. (See Fig. 1)

Stitch together a green, light yellow/cream, red, cream, green strip (See Fig. 2) then sew this to the right side of the Fig. 1 piece.

Stitch together red and light yellow/cream 1 ½" squares, alternating colors, and sew to the left hand side of the 4 ¼" black square.

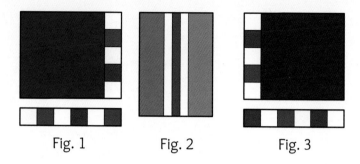

Fig. 1   Fig. 2   Fig. 3

Sew together 6 red and light yellow/cream 1 ½" squares, alternating colors, and sew to the bottom of the piece you just made.

This completes the top row of your block.

Next stitch the center row:

Fig. 4 and 6 are the same. Stitch as follows: 1 green, light yellow/cream, red, light yellow/cream, green strips to make this section. Make 2 of these.

Fig. 5 is a black 3 ¾" square. Sew these sections together to make the middle row. Sew the top row onto this section.

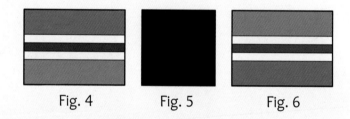

Fig. 4   Fig. 5   Fig. 6

The bottom row has the same components as the top row, but notice that the 1 ½" squares are sewn on the right and top side on the first block (Fig. 7) and on the left and top on the second one (Fig. 9).

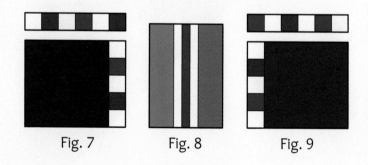

Fig. 7   Fig. 8   Fig. 9

Sew all 3 of these rows together and you've completed one block. (See Fig. 10) If you want your quilt to be the same size as mine, make 12 more of these blocks.

Fig. 10

HALF BLOCKS
Make 8

For each of the half blocks cut:
* 1 black 6 ³/₈" square; cut diagonally once to make 2 triangles for each half block.
* 1 black 5 ⅞" square cut once diagonally to get 2 triangles – you need 1 square for each half block.
* 4 green 1 ⅝" x 4 ⅞" strips for each half block
* 4 light yellow/cream ⅞" x 4 ⅞" strips for each half block
* 1 black 4 ⅛" square for each half block
* 2 red ⅞" x 4 ⅞" strips for each half block

The instructions for sewing the half blocks are the same as for the whole blocks, with the exception that the half blocks have one black 4 ⅛" square and the others will be triangles.

After you make 2 of the red/cream/green units and the red/cream squares you can stitch them in rows as shown below.

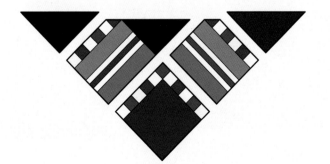

CORNER BLOCKS
Make 4

For each of the corner blocks cut:
* 1 black 6 ³/₈" square and cut diagonally twice to make 4 triangles, 2 per corner block
* 1 black 3 ¼" square, cut once diagonally to make 2 triangles, 1 per corner block
* 2 red 1 ⅛" x 1 ¾" wide polygon (template A) per corner block
* 5 red 1 ¼ inch squares per corner block
* 6 light yellow/cream 1 ¼" squares per corner block
* 2 green 1 ⅝" x 4 ⅞" strips for each corner block
* 2 light yellow/cream ⅞" x 4 ⅞" strips for each corner block
* 2 red ⅞" x 4 ⅞" strips for each corner block

Cut 2 red 1 ⅛" x 1 ¾" wide polygon (template A) per block according to the corner block cutting instructions above. All the other pieces can be rotary cut, but you will notice that these are not square, so use the template shown here to complete the corners of your blocks.

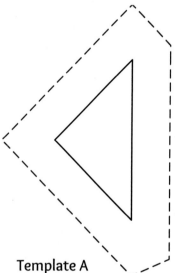

Template A

Stitch this corner unit the same as before. Stitch a Template A triangle onto each side of a striped unit and outside edge as shown below.

After completing all your whole blocks, half blocks and corner blocks, stitch them together in diagonal rows as follows:

Row 1: this is a corner – you can add this after you make the second diagonal row
Row 2: half block, whole block, half block
Row 3: half block 3 whole blocks, half block
Row 4: corner, 5 whole blocks, corner
Row 5: half block, 3 whole blocks, half block
Row 6: half block, whole block, half block
Row 7: add the final corner block

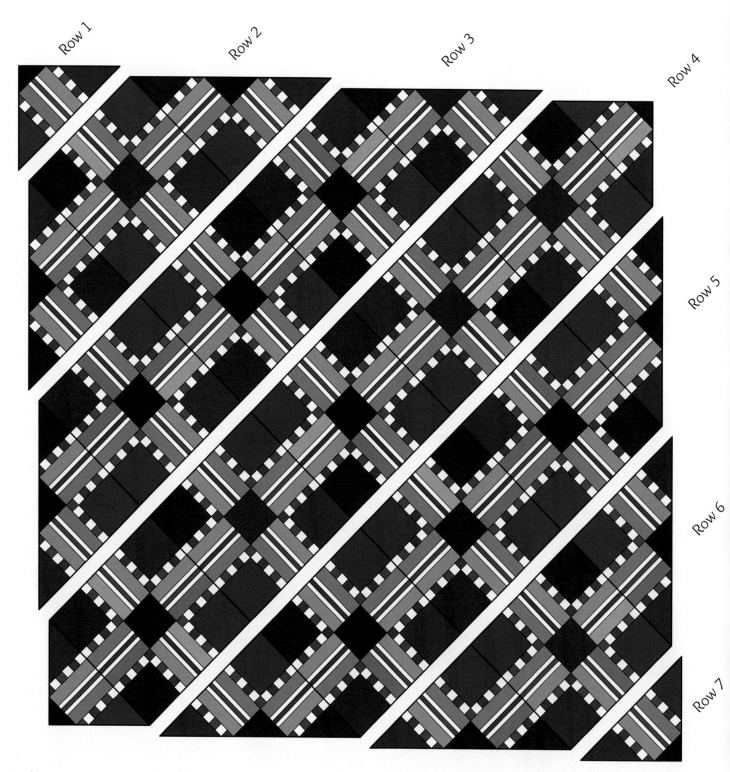

You've completed the top for this quilt. Your neighborhood is in place and you can track Santa's Route.

BORDERS

To keep the theme of a neighborhood going, the first border on this quilt looks like some of the bigger roads around town.

Cut 1 ⅝" strips of assorted reds and light yellow/creams. Stitch a red strip between 2 of the light yellow/cream strips to make this border strip. It should measure 3 ⅞" wide when the strips are all sewn together.

Cut 4 – 3 ⅞" black post blocks. After measuring the border lengths of YOUR quilt, stitch enough of these strips together to go across your quilt, minus the post block. Add these borders to the top and bottom of your quilt.

Now, measure down through the middle of your quilt to get an accurate measurement of the length of your quilt and add the black post blocks to each end for the sides.

BINDING

Since Santa arrives during the night, by the time you get to the binding all the lights in your neighborhood should be out. Keeping the theme of a night ride, I chose to use an assortment of blacks for the binding.

Cut 2" strips of various blacks and sew them together. Add up the total of all 4 sides of your quilt, plus an additional 15" to finish off your binding.

So, did you get to see Santa arrive? I've never been able to do that! I always fall asleep. Perhaps that's why I still believe.

Making all the components first, then assembling the different blocks together makes this one easier than it looks. Well, perhaps not as quickly as other simpler blocks, but look what you have accomplished.

Good job!

The outer border of this quilt reminds me of the bigger highways leading into town. It's wider and has only two post blocks.

Cut 4 ½" strips of assorted greens. Stitch them together after getting the measurement of your quilt.

Cut 2 black – 4 ½" post blocks

To the bottom left and the top right borders I stitched on a post block then measured up through the middle of my quilt to get an accurate measurement for them. Refer to the photo for placement.

As a child I can remember hearing stories from my mom about working a little extra so that my sister and I could have a better Christmas. One year she was so proud that with the money she made, they were able to purchase special dolls and doll buggies for my sister and me. Mom didn't have a doll when she was growing up so she thought it was very important that we did. My sister Sharron's doll had dark hair and her buggy looked just like the pram mom had for us. My doll had blonde hair and she had a pink tin buggy with big wheels.

We were never allowed to run out into the living room, where the Christmas tree was, on Christmas morning until both of our parents were with us. They wanted to see the look on our faces. Of course, to two little girls that were so excited, it seemed like it took forever for them to get ready. Mom would turn on all the lights and dad had to have the movie camera in hand to film all the excitement. We would jump up and down, trying to encourage our parents to hurry up! After what seemed like hours, we were allowed to run down the hall to see what Santa had brought. Much to mom's disappointment, we ran right to our stockings. It was much later, after everything in the stocking was taken out, that we saw the dolls and buggies. Christmas was always made special at our house.

For your special Christmas, let me introduce you to...

Quilt Size: 40" x 50"
Block Size: 10" square, finished

Christmas Packages

Designed and Stitched by: Lynda Hall
Machine Quilted by: Katherine Christenson

Gather together the following items and let's get started:

FABRICS AND SUPPLIES

❄ $7/8$ yard assorted light yellows (creams) for background squares and post blocks
❄ 2 yards assorted greens for background squares and outer border
❄ $1/3$ yard assorted blacks for bows and ribbons
❄ $2/3$ yard assorted reds for bows, ribbons and inner border

NOTE: You will need ribbons for several of the bows (refer to picture for placement)

Templates are on page 89.

CUTTING INSTRUCTIONS

❋ Cut 6 – light yellow (cream) 10 ½" background squares
❋ Cut 6 – green 10 ½" background squares

❋ Cut 5 Green bows – Template A
❋ Cut 4 Red bows – Template A
❋ Cut 1 light yellow (cream) bow – Template A

❋ Cut 20 Black triangle pieces – Template B
❋ Cut 8 green triangles pieces – Template B
❋ Cut 4 red triangles pieces – Template B
❋ Cut 8 yellow (middle value cream) triangle pieces – Template B

❋ Cut 10 Template C circles – 5 red and 5 black

❋ Cut 6 – 1 ½" x 10 ½" strips red for ribbons
❋ Cut 4 – 1 ½" x 10 ½" strips black for ribbons
❋ Cut 2 – 1 ½" x 10 ½" strips green for ribbons
❋ Cut 2 – 1 ¾" x 10 ½" strips for the package without the bow

Refer to the picture for placement of the different colored packages.

After you cut all the pieces you will need for the background squares it's time to appliqué it all down.

RIBBONS

Some of the packages have ribbons going both vertically and horizontally ... some have none. It's easiest to appliqué these ribbons, and also the bows, on your squares before you sew the blocks together.

Fold the 10 ½" square in half both ways to find the center of your block. (See Fig. 1)

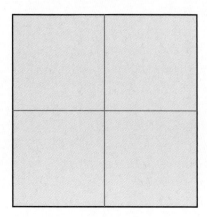

Fig. 1

Straddle the 1 ½" strip vertically; turn under ¼" on each side and stitch in place. Do the same thing horizontally across the block. (See Fig. 2)

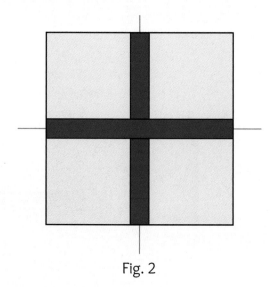

Fig. 2

BOWS

Templates for these shapes are on page 89. Add ¼" seam allowance to each one.

Appliqué the bow down after you have the ribbons in place. (See Fig. 3)

Fig. 3

Appliqué the diamond pieces on top of the bow, making sure the diamonds meet in the middle. (See Fig. 4)

Fig. 4

Stitch the center circle on top and your bow is complete. (See Fig. 5)

Fig. 5

The ribbons and bows will be done in various color combinations, so refer to the photo for placement. There are several that don't have the ribbons and one that has a ribbon, but no bow at all. However, this is your quilt so please feel free to make them any way you like.

When you have appliquéd all the squares, stitch them together in rows of 3 across and 4 down.

BORDERS

Small Inner Border
Cut 1 ½" strips of assorted reds for the inner border.

Cut 4 – 1 ½" light yellows (creams) for the post blocks.

I am a big fan of starting at the top of my quilt when adding borders, then moving along the right hand side, bottom, and left.

For each border you add, measure across and down through the middle of your quilt to get an accurate measurement.

Outer Border
Cut 4 ½" strips of a green plaid for the outside borders.

Cut 4 ½" light yellows (creams) for the post blocks.

Again, measure across and down through the middle of your quilt to get an accurate measurement for each one you add.

BINDING
To frame this wall hanging I chose to use an assortment of reds stitched together. Cut these strips 2" wide, fold in half, press and you're ready to add them onto the outside of your quilt.

This turns out to be a good-sized wall hanging and I know the exact spot where mine will hang during the Christmas holidays. The stairwell seems the perfect place for me. Everyone that comes in will be able to see it hanging there.

NOTE: Perhaps name tags with your family members on them would be fun pinned to the packages. The tags could also be embroidered.

After Santa has arrived and all the packages have been opened and enjoyed, it's off to the kitchen for me. In a few short hours all the family that can make it (I believe we number 31 at the present time) start arriving. Like decorating early to have the house as festive as I can, I start preparing Christmas dinner several days in advance, too. I've been cooking dinner for our family at least 37 years now and can't see it any other way. Although we don't have goose for Christmas, it's what my gramma would have served, so thought this fun quilt with the flying geese running through it should be called just that.

Let me introduce you to...

Quilt Size: 67" square
Block Size: 18"

Christmas Goose

Designed by: Lynda Hall
Stitched by: Donna Phillips and Lynda Hall
Machine Quilted by: Katherine Christenson

Gather together the following and let's get started:

FABRIC AND SUPPLIES
- ❄ 3 ⅜ yards total – assorted reds
- ❄ ⅞ yard total – assorted greens for sashing and border
- ❄ ⅝ yard total – assorted light yellows (creams)
- ❄ ⅝ yard total – assorted blue, orange, purple, dark yellow (brown), green, black for half square triangles
- ❄ 1 ⅞ yards total – assorted blacks for blocks and border

These blocks are on point so you will be making two types of blocks; whole blocks and half blocks. Because the half blocks reach out to the outside corners, you don't have to make corner blocks. Templates are on pages 90-92.

WHOLE BLOCKS
Make 4

For each of the whole blocks cut:
- ❄ 4 assorted red Template A pieces
- ❄ 4 assorted black Template B pieces
- ❄ Cut 4 assorted green Template C pieces
- ❄ 4 green 2 ⅛" x 8 ⅝" strips for the sashing
- ❄ 5 red 2 ⅛" square – 1 for the middle, 4 for each corner

- ❄ 6 – 3 ⅝" squares in assorted colors – blue, orange, purple, dark yellow (brown), green, black. Cut diagonally twice to get 4 triangles for the half square triangles. Label these triangles "D".
- ❄ 4 light yellow (assorted creams) 3 ⅝" squares; cut diagonally twice to get 16 light yellow (cream) triangles for each full block. Label these triangles "E".
- ❄ 2 light yellow (cream) 3 ¼" squares; cut diagonally once to get 4 triangles from 2 squares for each block. Label these triangles "F".

Start making your block by sewing the template B piece to the Template A piece. Make 4 of these for each of the whole blocks – 16 total

1. Fold each Template A and B pieces in half to find the center.

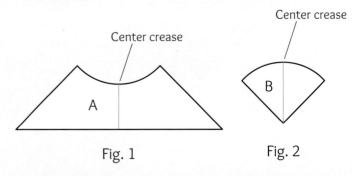

Fig. 1

Fig. 2

2. Using two pins, pin the center of both pieces, right sides together. Also use two pins for each end. Using 2 pins in these places helps anchor the pieces in place until you can sew them down; pin in between. Sew

with the larger of the two pieces on top. This will assure you that no puckers happen ... why unsew if you don't have to?!

When sewn together, press the black B piece toward the larger red A piece.

3. For the 4 center pieces, first make these 4 units. Sew a cream D and a dark D piece together to make a half square triangle. Make 2 for each side. Add 1 more dark D piece to the right side. Add a cream E piece to the right end. Make sure the flat side of the E triangle is facing out or it won't fit. (See Fig. 3)

Fig. 3

Make two of these units for each of the 4 green C pieces – and to one of them add a red F square at the end as shown in Fig. 4. It will look like this when you have completed this section.

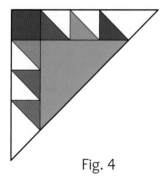

Fig. 4

These 4 units will be sewn to the 4 red/black centers you made earlier. This is how each of the completed units will look. (See Fig. 5)

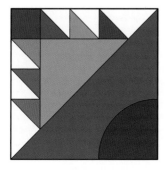

Fig. 5

Sew a green 2 ⅛" x 8 ⅝" sashing strip between two of the above units. Your red 2 ⅛" square should be at the outside edge. (See Fig. 6)

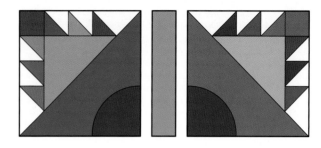

Fig. 6

Between the two units you've just made sew two green sashing strips with a red F square in the middle as shown. (See Fig. 7)

Fig. 7

Then add the remaining two units to the other side and your block is complete. There are 4 whole blocks in this quilt. They are placed on point. If you want your quilt to be larger it's just a matter of making more blocks.

Fig. 8

HALF BLOCKS
Make 8

Because these blocks are on point, you will have to make half blocks to complete your quilt. There are no corner blocks in this one, so you only have to make 8 half blocks.

I have included templates for the half blocks so you don't waste material by making full sized blocks and then cutting them in half less the seam allowance.

For each of the half blocks cut:
* ❊ 8 red Whole Block Template A pieces
* ❊ 16 red Half Block Template A pieces
* ❊ 8 black Whole Block Template B pieces
* ❊ 16 black Half Block Template B pieces
* ❊ 8 green Whole Block Template C pieces
* ❊ 16 green Half Block Template C pieces
* ❊ 10 assorted dark Whole Block D pieces for the half-square triangles
* ❊ 8 assorted cream Whole Block D pieces for the half-square triangles
* ❊ 1 red 3 ⅝" square; cut twice diagonally to make 4 triangles. You will only use 3.

You construct the half blocks as you did the whole blocks, except you will be using different sized pieces for part of it.

Below is what it will look like when all the pieces are sewn together.

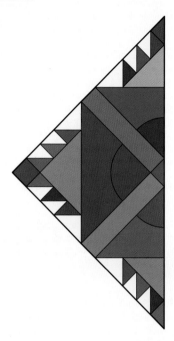

When you have completed the 4 whole blocks and 8 half blocks they will be sewn together in diagonal rows:

Row 1 – two half blocks sewn together with the half-square triangles towards each other making the geese

Row 2 – one half block, two whole blocks, one additional half block

Row 3 – one half block, two whole blocks, one additional half block

Row 4 – two half blocks sewn together with the half square triangles towards each other making the geese

The center of your top is completed! Yay!

BORDERS

There are 3 borders on this quilt. I know, why three? When you look at the quilt you will see 3 different sized squares. I liked the way it looked on paper. Although they don't complete the geese out to the edge, it made me feel like it complimented the center.

Border 1

The small green border completes the lattice work between the blocks, so kept it the same green color.

- ❋ Cut 2" strips of assorted greens and stitch them together for all 4 sides

- ❋ Cut 4 assorted cream post blocks for the corners

Border 2

- ❋ Cut 3 ½" strips out of one black star print for this second border

- ❋ Cut 3 ½" assorted cream post blocks for this border

Border 3

- ❋ Cut 4 ¼" assorted red strips, stitch together for this border

- ❋ Cut 4 ¼" assorted cream post blocks for this border

For each of these borders, remember to always measure across and/or down through the middle of your quilt for an accurate measurement. We all stitch differently so your border lengths could be different than mine.

If you put your borders on top/bottom then both sides … the measurement you get would be the same for the top and bottom, and the same for both sides, which would also include the top and bottom borders.

IF you add your borders by going around the quilt, then you would have to include the measurement of each border you add. I personally like to add them going around the quilt, but please do this the way you feel comfortable.

BINDING

The quilt is 67" square … to figure the total inches multiply the 67" x 4 and that gives you the amount you need … 268". To get an accurate measurement for your quilt binding, measure down through the center of each border strip, not at the edge. Multiply that number by 4 and add 15" more for finishing off the ends. For my quilt I needed 283".

Your quilt top is complete.

Well, everyone should be here soon. It's another year of family and fun times together. My mom turned 89 this year and I'm so glad she's still with us for another Christmas holiday! I hope everyone saves room for the homemade bread pudding and/or the pumpkin pie Donna always brings.

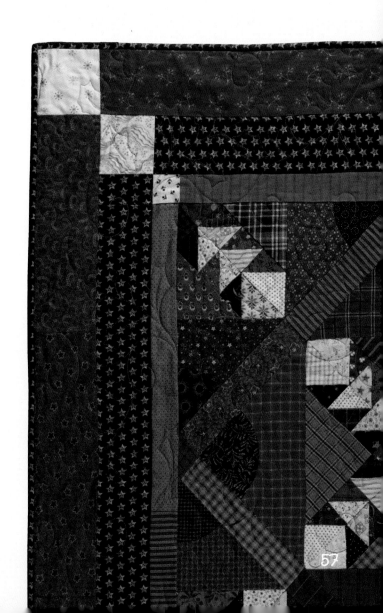

Christmas continues to be fun when you have a quilt that can be hung for Christmas and then stay for a while. I'm always sad when I take down all the trees and put away the Santas. What I do like is that all the snowmen can stay out during the rest of the winter months because ... brrrr, baby it's still cold outside! Now, think of a quilt that has been hung by the chimney with care — that doesn't have to be put away. If I recall, another day to celebrate is just around the corner. You know, it's the one that has "Love" in mind. That's right, Valentine's Day! This non-traditional Christmas quilt would be a perfect one to hang when Valentine's Day rolls around.

Let me introduce you to ...

Quilt Size: 66" square
Block Size: 12 ¹/₂" square

Bridging the Gap

Designed and Stitched by: Lynda Hall
Machine Quilted by: Katherine Christenson

Gather together the following and let's get started:

FABRIC AND SUPPLIES
- ❋ 2 ⅛ yards total assorted reds
- ❋ 2 ½ yards total assorted light yellows (creams)
- ❋ ⅝ yard total assorted dark yellows (brown)
- ❋ ¾ yard total assorted blacks.

This quilt was constructed with the blocks on point. Having blocks on point means making a few different types of blocks; whole blocks, half blocks and corner blocks.

Let's start putting the blocks together.

WHOLE BLOCKS
Make 13

For each of the whole blocks cut:
- ❋ 4 assorted dark yellow (brown) 3 ½" squares
- ❋ 1 black 3 ½" square
- ❋ 4 assorted middle value yellow (creams) 3 ½" squares
- ❋ 2 assorted light yellow (lt. cream) 4 ¼" squares; cut diagonally twice to make 8 triangles
- ❋ 2 assorted middle value yellows (slightly darker reams) 4 ½" squares; cut diagonally twice to make 8 triangles
- ❋ 4 assorted red 4 ½" squares; cut diagonally twice to make 16 triangles
- ❋ 1 black 4 ¼" squares; cut twice diagonally to make 4 triangles

Start by sewing the 3 ½" squares together for the middle row in this order: (See Fig. 1)

For each block cut:
- ❋ 1 light yellow (cream)
- ❋ 1 dark yellow (brown)
- ❋ 1 black
- ❋ 1 dark yellow (brown)
- ❋ 1 light yellow (cream)

Then add the black triangles onto each end.

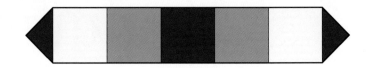

Fig. 1

The top and bottom rows will be stitched together as follows:
- ❋ 1 dark yellow (brown) square
- ❋ 1 light yellow (cream) square
- ❋ 8 light yellow (cream) triangles
- ❋ 4 middle value yellow (slightly darker cream)
- ❋ 8 assorted red triangles

Sew the dark yellow (brown) and light yellow (cream) square together .

Add the black triangle to the outside edge near the light yellow (cream) square.

Sew 2 light yellow (cream) triangles together along the short side.

Sew 2 red/middle value yellow (slightly darker cream) triangles together making 2 half-square triangle blocks. The reds should be on the outside edge when you sew them together.

Sew these two units together as shown in the diagram.

Sew a red triangle onto each end.

You will make 2 of these units for each of the whole blocks. (See Fig. 2)

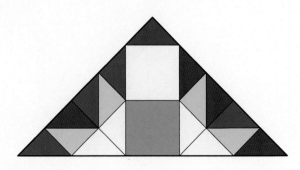

Fig. 2

Sew one of each of these units onto the middle row and you have one whole block. If you are making your quilt the size of mine, you will make 12 more of these blocks.

HALF BLOCKS
Make 8

The half blocks are constructed the same way with a couple size changes. Because you are literally splitting a whole block in half, the center squares become rectangles and the outside edge triangles become smaller. Everything else is the same and sewn together in rows like the whole blocks. (Fig. 3)

Cut:
* 1 black 2" x 3 ½" rectangle
* 2 dark yellow (brown) 2" x 3 ½" rectangles
* 2 light yellow (cream) 2" x 3 ½" rectangles
* 1 black 2 ⅜" square; cut diagonally once to make 2 triangles

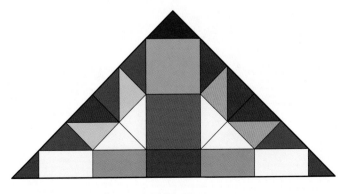

Fig. 3

CORNER BLOCKS
Make 4

The Corner blocks have the same size pieces as the half blocks. (Fig. 4)

For each corner block cut:
* 2 dark yellow (brown) 2" x 3 ½" rectangles
* 2 light yellow (cream) 2" x 3 ½" rectangles
* 1 light yellow (cream) 4 ¼" square; cut diagonally twice to make 4 triangles
* 1 middle value yellow (slightly darker cream) 4 ¼" square; cut diagonally twice to make 4 triangles (you will have two left over for another corner)
* 1 red 4 ¼" squares; cut diagonally twice to make 4 triangles
* 1 black 2 ⅜" square; cut once diagonally to make 2 triangles
* 1 black 2" square

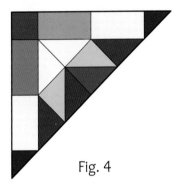

Fig. 4

When you have made all 13 whole blocks, 8 half blocks and 4 corner blocks it's time to sew them all together.

I like to pin all the blocks to my design wall, but if you don't have one, you can lay them out on the floor to see how they all look before stitching them together. Moving them around to see how you like them best, of course, should be done at this point. Un-sewing isn't a favorite thing for me, so stepping back and viewing them now makes everything easier.

A sure way to see if you like what you've done is to stand with your back to your design wall and look at your blocks through a mirror. It's one the fastest ways to see if something is not in the right place. This is a trick I used to teach my art students when they were painting. Your eye will spot a mistake in a second with this reverse view.

SEW THE BLOCKS TOGETHER

These blocks are on point so they are sewn together
in diagonal rows, as shown in the diagram. (Fig. 5)

Fig. 5

BORDERS
There are 2 borders on this quilt.

Inner Border
Cut 1 ½" strips of assorted black for the small inner border.

Outer Border
The outside border is called a dogtooth border. I love the way it frames the center of the quilt. What is important to remember is that NOT ALL the triangles are evenly sized. The A and C pieces are different sizes and the D piece is longer than the B pieces. However, when you first look at it, they all appear the same.

There are three sections on each side of the quilt (12 sections for the entire quilt) and it has post blocks in each of the corners. Here is what you need to cut (templates for A & C are on page 94; templates for B & D are on page 93).

For each section cut:
* A – 1 red 4 ⅝" x 6 ½" rectangle; cut diagonally once to make 2 triangles – this can be rotary cut and doesn't need a template but I made one for you anyway
* B – 1 red 9 ⅞" x 6 ⅛" rectangle; use template provided to cut this section
* C – 1 red 6 ⅛" x 6 ⅜" rectangle; cut once diagonally to make 2 triangles – this is also rotary cut so doesn't need a template, but I made one for you just the same
* D – 2 light yellow (cream) 9 ⅞" x 6 ⅛" rectangles; use template provided to cut this section

Post Blocks: Cut 4 – 5 ½" squares, 2 dark yellow (brown) and 2 red

After you have all 12 sections made, sew together 3 for each of the 4 sides of your quilt. Stitch one of the 3 sections to the top and bottom of your quilt top.

Sew a post block to each end of the remaining borders. Stitch these to the sides and you have a finished quilt top.

Normally when you finish a quilt, you make a back for it. But, this one's a little different. This quilt is a reversible quilt. The holiday after Valentine's Day is St. Patrick's Day ... and yes, I'm a little Irish so I would be hard pressed not to have a special quilt for this holiday. Let's see, this one's been out for Christmas, Valentine's Day and can still stay around for yet another month. I love the time span on this one.

NOTE: If you choose to keep this quilt separate, feel free to make a pieced back with something fun on it and call it finished.

Log Cabin quilts have been around for a very long time. It's one of my all time favorite blocks to make. How the blocks are sewn together makes all the difference in the look of the quilt, but I have several that are stitched just like this one, all in different colors, and all very special.

I have a picture of my mom's family in front of their log cabin; perhaps that's why I love these quilts so much. Used as the back for Bridging the Gap, it makes for a delightful reversible quilt. Remember Christmas comes and goes so fast that if we have quilts that can stay out for the holiday right next to it, we don't have to change out the quilts quite as often. So from Christmas into Valentine's Day and then St. Patrick's Day we've covered three holidays with one quilt. It doesn't get any better than that.

Let me introduce you to ...

Quilt Size: 66" square
Block Size: 8" square

Behind the Log Cabin

Designed and Stitched by: Lynda Hall
Machine Quilted by: Katherine Christenson

Gather together the following items and let's get started:

FABRICS AND SUPPLIES

❋ ½ yard assorted reds for block centers and inner border
❋ 1 yard total assorted greens for blocks
❋ 2 ⅞ yards total assorted light yellows (creams) for blocks and outer borders

CUTTING INSTRUCTIONS

You will cut the following for **each** of the 36 blocks (templates are provided on pages 95-96, or you can just cut these from 1 ½" strips)

A & B: 1 ½" square – one red, one cream
C & D: 1 ½" x 2 ½" – one cream, one green
E & F: 1 ½" x 3 ½" – one cream, one green
G & H: 1 ½" x 4 ½" – one cream, one green
I & J: 1 ½" x 5 ½" – one cream, one green
K & L: 1 ½" x 6 ½" – one cream, one green
M & N: 1 ½" x 7 ½" – one cream, one green
O: 1 ½" x 8 ½" – one green

PIECING THE BLOCKS

Sew pieces A (red) and B (cream) together; sew C to one side to make a square. Going around the block and following the illustration below, sew the strips alphabetically, making sure all the cream pieces are on one side and the green pieces are on the other.

The placement of the blocks, called "setting", determines how a log cabin quilt looks. They can be stitched together in straight furrows, a sunshine and shadows pattern; they can be sewn into pineapple variations, courthouse steps and many more. I love each of them in their own way, but thought the Barn Raising setting would be best for this quilt since my family were farmers and actually did go to many barn raisings in their town.

As I completed the blocks I placed them on my design wall in the setting I wanted to use. I sewed the blocks together in rows, and then sewed the rows together. 36 blocks later, I had the middle of my St. Patrick's Day, barn raising, Behind the Cabin quilt center finished. Whew!

BORDERS

Inner Border

Cut 1 ½" strips of assorted reds for this inner border and then stitch them together.

To get an accurate measurement for a border, always measure across and/or down through the middle of your quilt. This will give you the correct length you need for each one you add.

When you get the desired length, fold your border strip in half and make a crease; fold your quilt top in half and mark the middle. Pin your border to your quilt top in the middle. Pin each end of the border strip at the outside edge of your quilt and work the rest in by pinning in place.

Do the same for the other two sides and your inner border is in place.

Outer Border

If you are going to make this quilt to stand alone, rather than back it with another quilt, cut your border fabric 8 ½" wide x the width and/or length of your top measuring down through the middle. A post block or three could be added to this border if you choose. You would cut them 8 ½" square. Also, post blocks don't have to be put in each of the corners … perhaps on this one they could be in the middle of the border all the way around.

If you plan to back this quilt with another quilt like I did, please follow these instructions:

It's important to know that whatever the size your border is going to end up — in this case 8" finished, you need to add at least an additional 4" around the outside edge because if you are going to have a machine quilter quilt your finished quilt, she will need that extra fabric for attaching it to the frame on her machine. The quilt "Bridging the Gap" (on page 61) is 66" square, including the borders. This quilt measures 66" square as well, so adding another 4" to your borders for "Behind the Log Cabin" means your border strips will be 12" all the way around.

You will see that this particular border is extra large and very plain. I decided to keep the cabin blocks to

36, but if you wish, you could make an additional row all the way around. It would mean making 28 additional log cabin blocks. It would also mean your border would be much smaller when finished.

Because this is on the back of another quilt, again, you don't have to make a back … Oh, I love the idea of reversible quilts. Changing quilts, especially if they are hung on a wall is a lot of work. I love that I can turn a quilt over and viola … there's another one! Besides, two quilts and one quilting is something I can really like.

When you have two quilts back to back, it's important to remember to have an overall quilting design that will enhance both sides. If the blocks are different sizes, as in this case, overall loops and stars were sewn to enhance both sides. I love stars and if it takes loops to get to the next one, then so be it.

Until next time,

Lynda

Sources

There are so many shops that now carry my pattern line, both here in the U.S.A. and abroad. I am very grateful to each of them. Together we can continue to make the quilting industry strong. If your local quilt shops don't carry my patterns or the materials needed to make them, perhaps introducing the shop owner to what you enjoy making can make a difference.

FABRIC COMPANIES AND DISTRIBUTORS

Moda/United Notions – graciously provides a lot of the fabrics I use in my quilts and they have distributed my pattern line since the beginning

Checker's Distributors – carries my patterns

WOOL
Blackberry Primitives
1944 High Street
Lincoln, NE 68502
www.blackberryprimitives.com

Heaven's to Betsy
46 Route 23
Claverack, NY 12513
www.heavens-to-betsy.com

Shakerwood Woolens
Rock Hill, South Carolina
www.shakerwoodwoolens.com

Weeks Dye Works
1510-103 Mechanical Blvd.
Garner, NC 27529
www.weeksdyeworks.com

Anita White
12835 Perry
Overland Park, KS 66213
913-685-0180
anitawhite.blogspot.com

THREAD
Weeks Dye Works cotton thread
1510-103 Mechanical Blvd.
Garner, North Carolina 27529
www.weeksdyeworks.com

Aurifil Wool Thread
www.aurifil.com

Templates

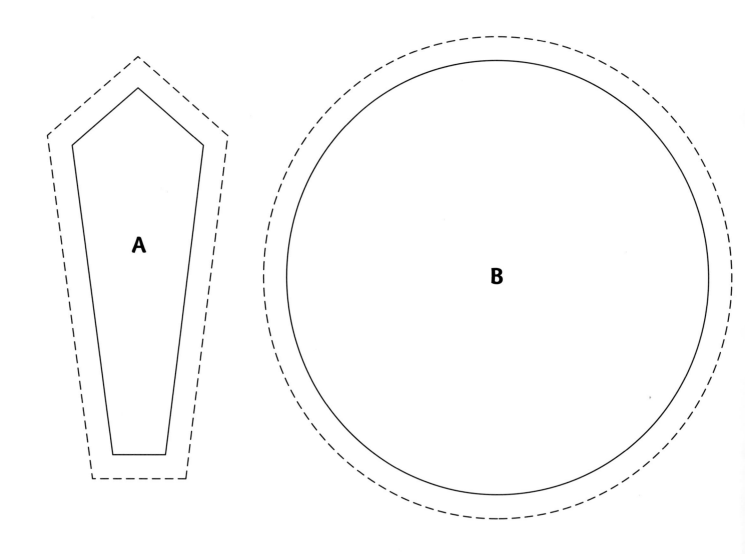

A

B

Christmas Wreaths

Chilly

Join template here

▲ Join template here ▲

Chilly

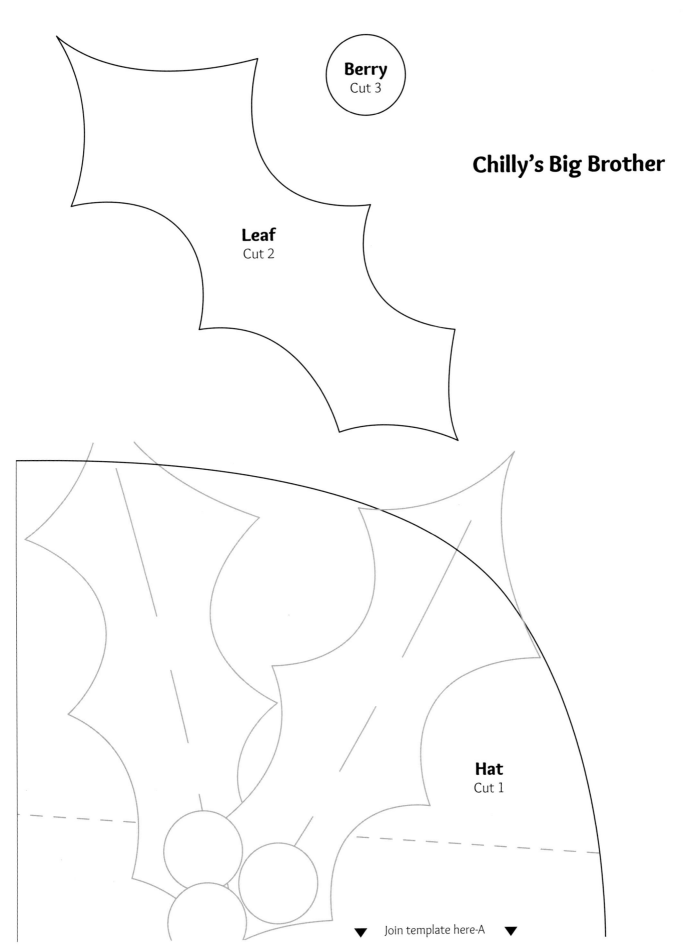

Berry
Cut 3

Chilly's Big Brother

Leaf
Cut 2

Hat
Cut 1

▼ Join template here-A ▼

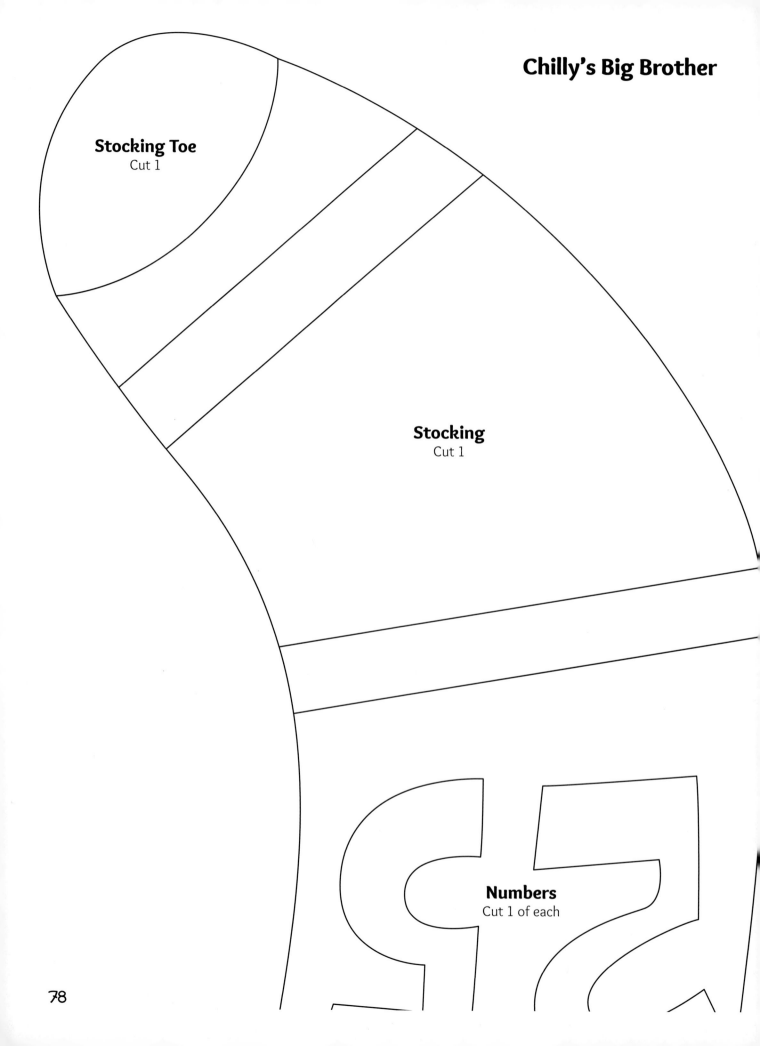

Chilly's Big Brother

Stocking Toe
Cut 1

Stocking
Cut 1

Numbers
Cut 1 of each

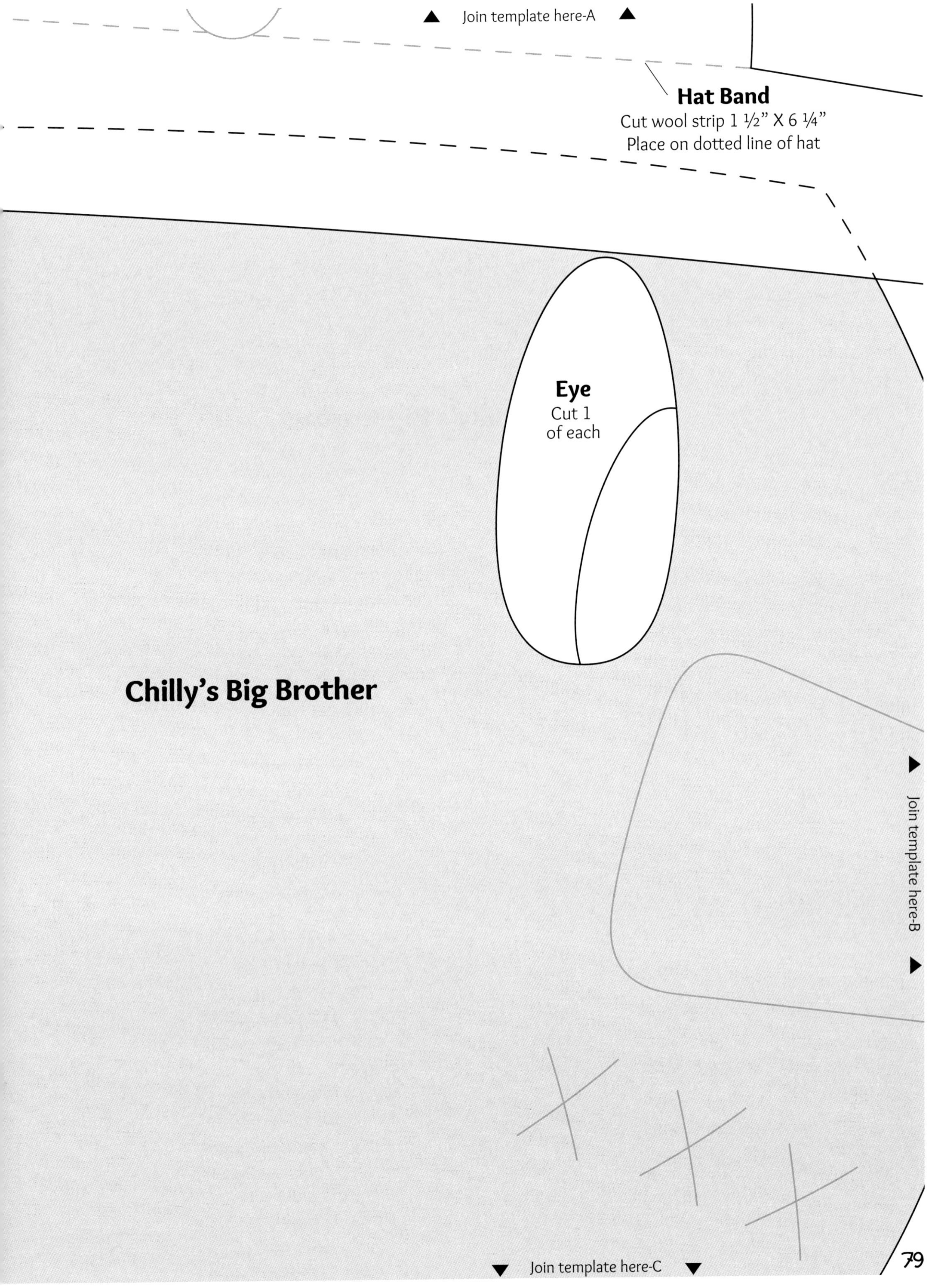

▲ Join template here-A ▲

Hat Band
Cut wool strip 1 ½" X 6 ¼"
Place on dotted line of hat

Eye
Cut 1
of each

Chilly's Big Brother

Join template here-B
▶
▶

▼ Join template here-C ▼

Chilly's Big Brother

Star
Cut 1

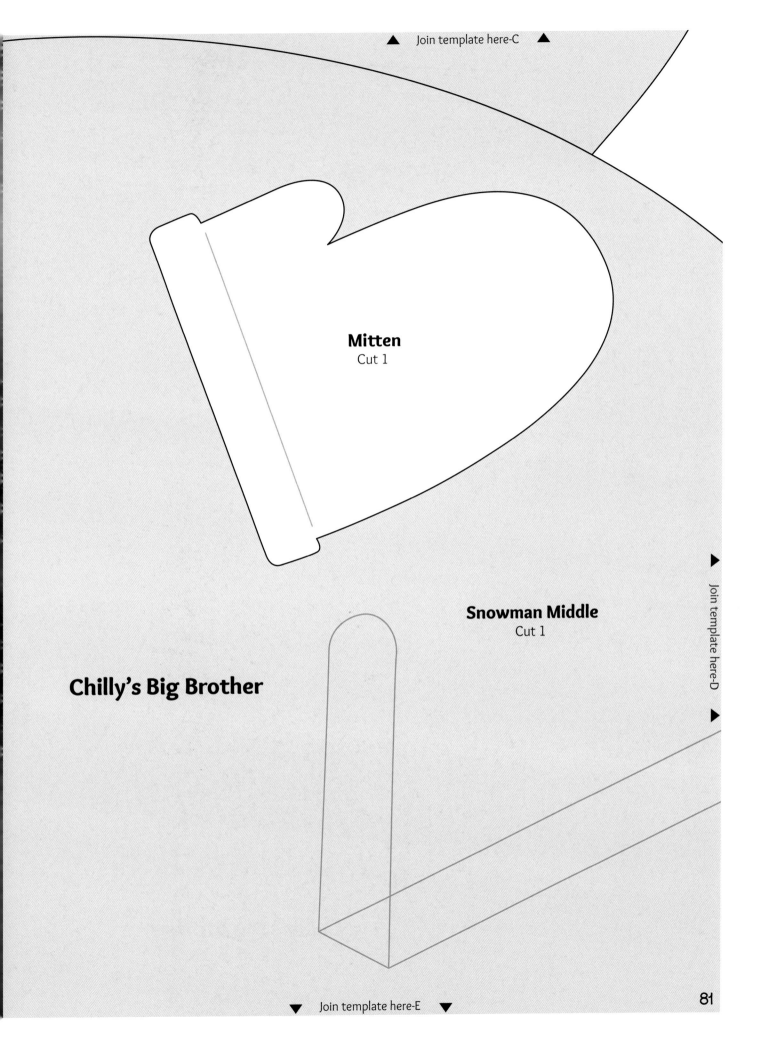

▲ Join template here-C ▲

Mitten
Cut 1

▶

Join template here-D

▶

Snowman Middle
Cut 1

Chilly's Big Brother

▼ Join template here-E ▼

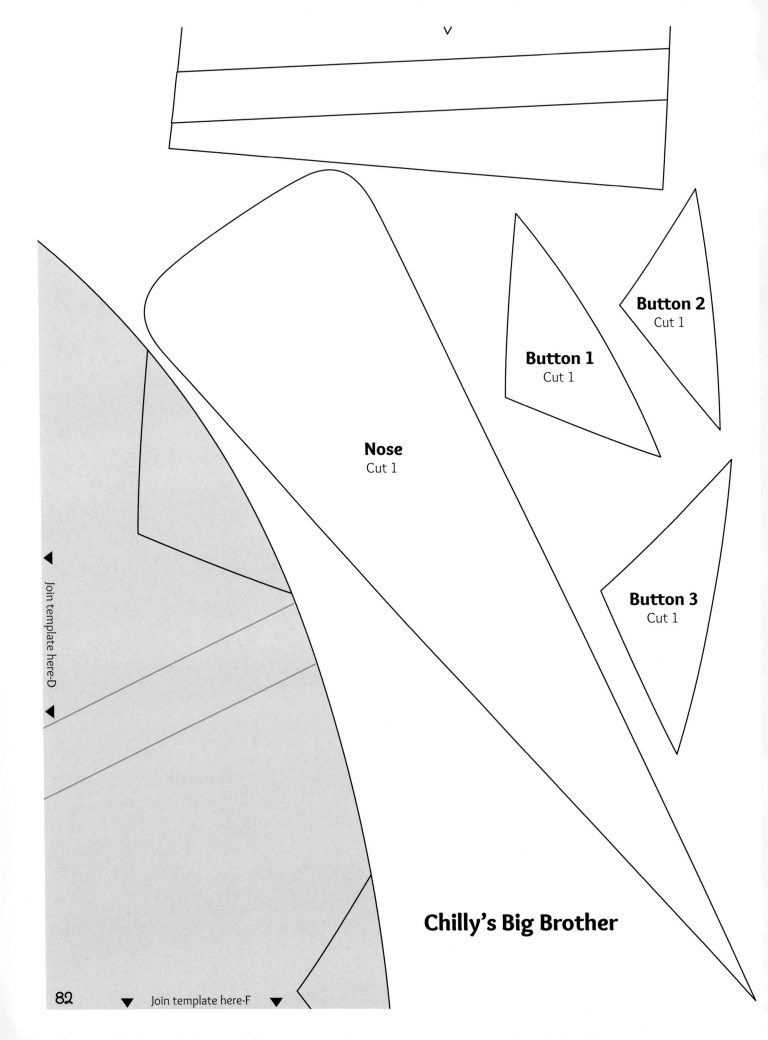

∨

Button 2
Cut 1

Button 1
Cut 1

Nose
Cut 1

Button 3
Cut 1

Chilly's Big Brother

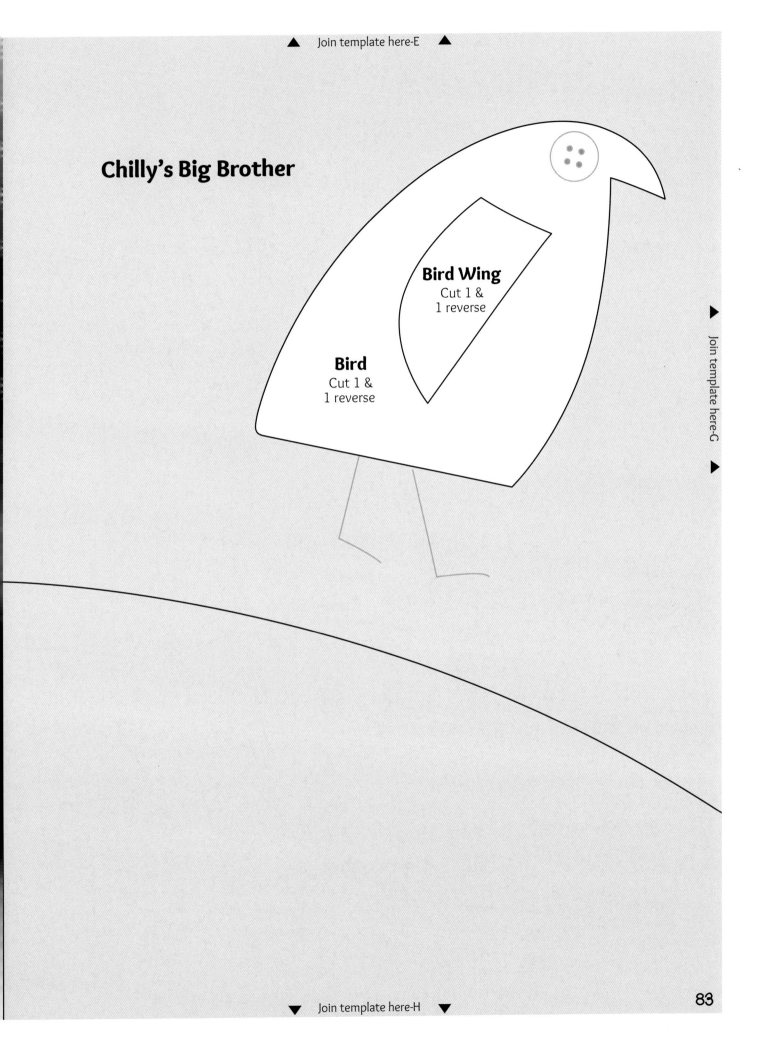

Chilly's Big Brother

Bird Wing
Cut 1 &
1 reverse

Bird
Cut 1 &
1 reverse

▲ Join template here-F ▲

▼ Join template here-I ▼

◀ Join template here-G ◀

Candy Cane
Cut 1

Candy Cane
Cut 1 & 1 reverse

Chilly's Big Brother

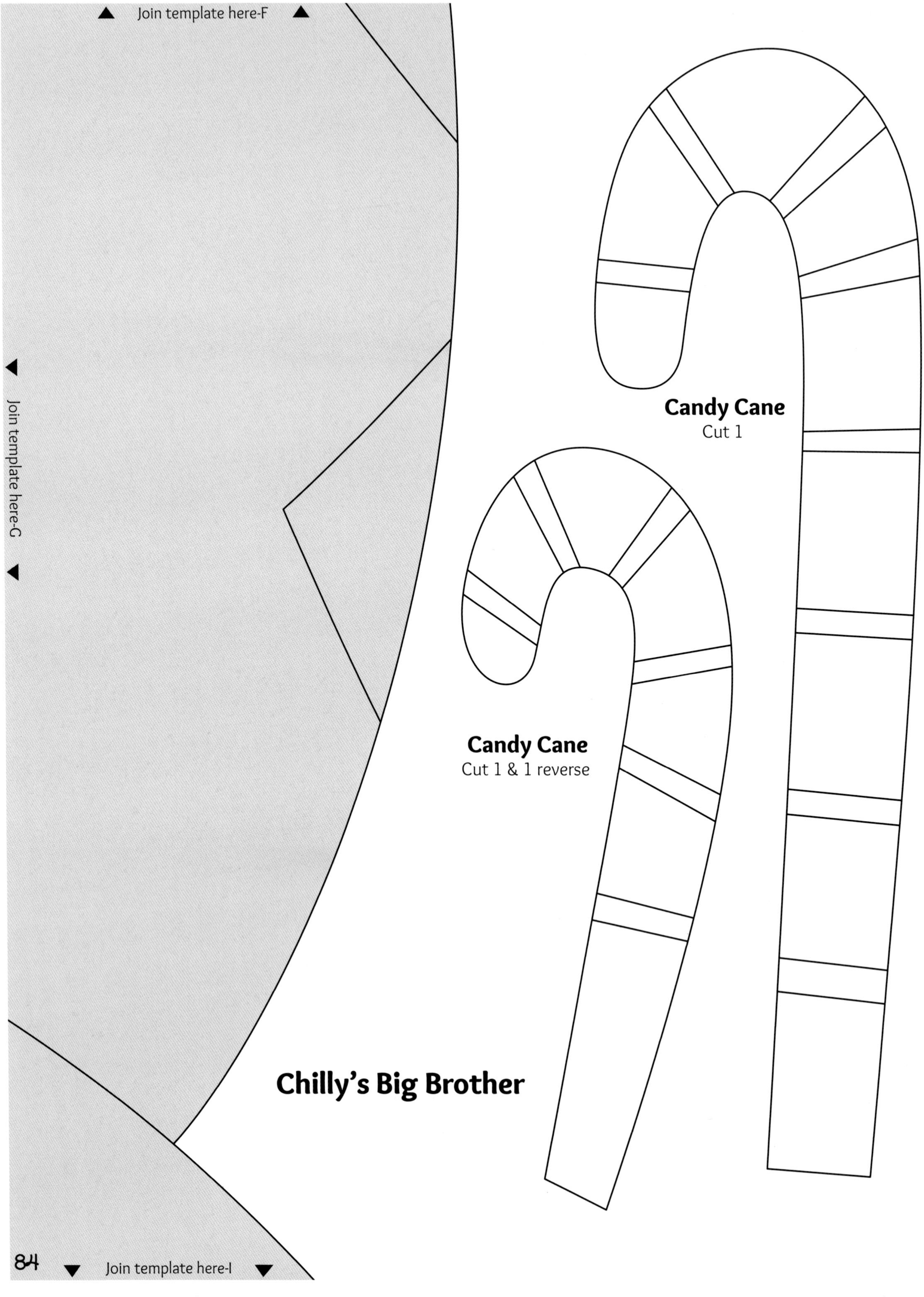